My Family

Mary Rose

Name _____

Age _____

Class _____

OXFORD

UNIVERSITY PRESS

OXFORD
UNIVERSITY PRESS

Great Clarendon Street, Oxford OX2 6DP

Oxford University Press is a department of the University of Oxford.
It furthers the University's objective of excellence in research, scholarship,
and education by publishing worldwide in

Oxford New York

Auckland Cape Town Dar es Salaam Hong Kong Karachi
Kuala Lumpur Madrid Melbourne Mexico City Nairobi
New Delhi Shanghai Taipei Toronto

With offices in

Argentina Austria Brazil Chile Czech Republic France Greece
Guatemala Hungary Italy Japan South Korea Poland Portugal
Singapore Switzerland Thailand Turkey Ukraine Vietnam

OXFORD and OXFORD ENGLISH are registered trade marks of
Oxford University Press in the UK and in certain other countries

ISBN 9780194400794

Printed in China

Commissioned photography by: Phil James

Illustration by: Mark Ruffle p 11

The publisher would like to thank the following for kind permimssion to reproduce photographs:
Stone pp 12, 15, 16 (Tim Davis)

With thanks to Sally Spray for her contribution to this series

The manufacturer's authorised representative in the EU for product safety is Oxford University Press España S.A.
of el Parque Empresarial San Fernando de Henares, Avenida de Castilla, 2 - 28830 Madrid (www.oup.es/en)

Reading Dolphins
Notes for teachers & parents

📖 Using the book

1 Begin by looking at the first story page (page 2). Look at the picture and ask questions about it. Then read the story text under the picture with your students. Use section 1 of the CD for this if possible.

2 Teach and check the understanding of any new vocabulary. Note that some of the words are in the **Picture Dictionary** at the back of the book.

3 Now look at the activities on the right-hand page. Show the example to the students and instruct them to complete the activities. This may be done individually, in pairs, or as a class.

4 Do the same for the remaining pages of the book.

5 Retell the whole story more quickly, reinforcing the new vocabulary. Sections 2 and 3 of the CD can help with this.

6 If possible, listen to the expanded story (section 4 of the CD). The students should follow in their books.

7 When the book is finished, use the **Picture Dictionary** to check that students understand and remember new vocabulary. Section 5 of the CD can help with this.

💿 Using the CD

The CD contains five sections.

1 The story told slowly, with pauses. Use this during the first reading. It may also be used for "Listen and repeat" activities at any point.

2 The story told at normal speed. This should be used once the students have read the book for the first time.

3 The story chanted. Students may want to chant along with the story.

4 The expanded story. The story is told in a longer version. This will help the students understand English when it is spoken faster, as they will now know the story and the vocabulary.

5 Vocabulary. Each word in the **Picture Dictionary** is spoken and then used in a simple sentence.

My name is May.
This is my family.

Number.

May $\boxed{5}$ father $\boxed{}$

brother $\boxed{}$ sister $\boxed{}$

mother $\boxed{}$

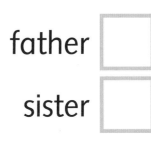

This is my father.
He is in the kitchen.

Read and circle.

① This is my father.
my mother. *(circled)*

② This is my sister.
my father.

③ This is my sister.
my brother.

④ This is my sister.
May.

⑤ This is my brother.
my mother.

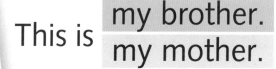

5

This is my mother.
She is in the living room.

Circle yes or no .

1. Can you see a telephone?

    (yes)   no

2. Can you see a TV?

    yes   no

3. Can you see a book?

    yes   no

4. Can you see flowers?

    yes   no

5. Can you see a cat?

    yes   no

6. Can you see an apple?

    yes   no

This is my brother, David.
He is in the bedroom.

Number.

poster **1**   window ☐

David ☐   books ☐

bed ☐   light ☐

This is my sister, Julie.
She is in the bathroom.

Number.

bathroom   1   kitchen   ☐

living room   ☐   bedroom   ☐

This is my dog, Jack.
And this is my cat, Jill.

What page?

① Julie is in the bathroom.

page  10

② Father is in the kitchen.

page

③ David is in the bedroom.

page

④ Mother is in the living room.

page

⑤ I can see a family.

page

This is my grandfather and this is my grandmother.

Connect.

brother •

cat •

dog •

sister •

grandfather •

grandmother •

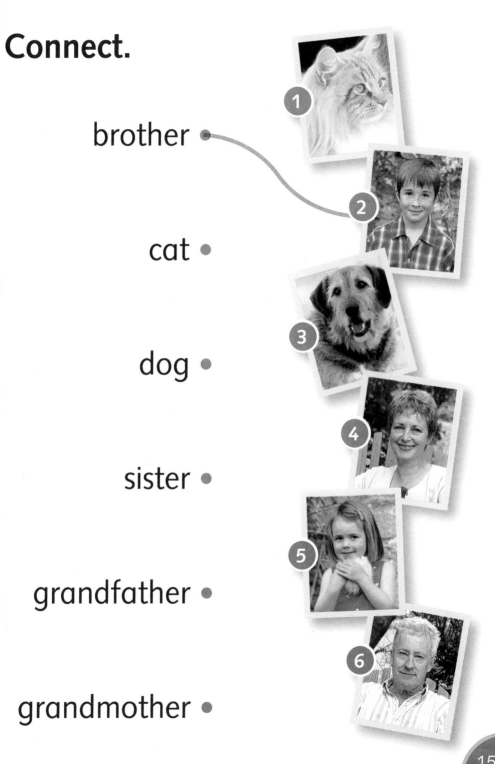

Picture Dictionary

bathroom

cat

bedroom

dog

blue

father

brother

grandfather

grandmother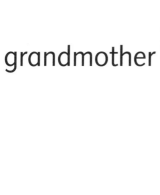

mother

green

red

kitchen

sister

living room

white

Dolphin Readers

Dolphin Readers are available at five levels, from Starter to 4.

The Dolphins series covers four major themes:

Grammar, Living Together, The World Around Us, Science and Nature.

For each theme, there are two titles at every level.

Activity Books are available for all Dolphins.

All Dolphins are available on audio CD.
(2 TITLES ON EACH CD ⊘ SEE TABLE BELOW)

Teacher's Notes are available at **www.oup.com/elt/dolphins**

	Grammar	Living Together	The World Around Us	Science and Nature
Starter	• Silly Squirrel • Monkeying Around ⊘	• My Family • A Day with Baby ⊘	• Doctor, Doctor • Moving House ⊘	• A Game of Shapes • Baby Animals ⊘
Level 1	• Meet Molly • Where Is It? ⊘	• Little Helpers • Jack the Hero ⊘	• On Safari • Lost Kitten ⊘	• Number Magic • How's the Weather? ⊘
Level 2	• Double Trouble • Super Sam ⊘	• Candy for Breakfast • Lost! ⊘	• A Visit to the City • Matt's Mistake ⊘	• Numbers, Numbers Everywhere • Circles and Squares ⊘
Level 3	• Students in Space • What Did You Do Yesterday? ⊘	• New Girl in School • Uncle Jerry's Great Idea ⊘	• Just Like Mine • Wonderful Wild Animals ⊘	• Things That Fly • Let's Go to the Rainforest ⊘
Level 4	• The Tough Task • Yesterday, Today and Tomorrow ⊘	• We Won the Cup • Up and Down ⊘	• Where People Live • City Girl, Country Boy ⊘	• In the Ocean • Go, Gorillas, Go ⊘